CHESTER TRAMWAYS

Barry M Marsden

Series editor by Robert J Harley

MP Middleton Press

Front cover photograph - see caption 66.

Back cover photograph - see caption 91.

Published May 2007

ISBN 978 1 906008 04 8

© *Middleton Press, 2007*

Design Deborah Esher

Published by
        Middleton Press
        Easebourne Lane
        Midhurst
        West Sussex
        GU29 9AZ
Tel: 01730 813169
Fax: 01730 812601
Email: info@middletonpress.co.uk
www.middletonpress.co.uk

Printed & bound by Biddles Ltd, Kings Lynn

HORSE CARS

ELECTRIC TRAMCARS

INTRODUCTION
AND ACKNOWLEDGEMENTS

The ancient city of Chester hosted both horse and electric trams, the first being a privately-run facility, opening on 10th June 1879, which ran from the General Railway Station to the suburb of Saltney on the Welsh border, a distance of 2.38 miles/3.8km, operating on a gauge of 4ft 8½in/1435mm. The electric tramway which superseded it began working on 6th April 1903 and followed the same route but on a gauge of 3ft 6in/1067mm to better accommodate the narrow streets in the city centre. An eastern extension to Boughton was opened on 22nd November 1906, lengthening the route mileage to 3.58/5.7km, but the undertaking always struggled for viability and the vehicles, of an out-of-date design even when new, were worn out by the late 1920s. They were replaced by motorbuses in February 1930.

The majority of photographs illustrating this album are published by kind permission of Chester History and Heritage, and I have to thank Alison Watson, Community Heritage Manager for her kind co-operation in making them available. Certain images from the Heritage collection, identified in the text, are published by kind permission of Frank Simpson, Chester Record Office, M. Rowlands, J. Garner and J. Clowes. Other pictures come via Geoffrey Smith, Cynthia Gent, Paul Knowles and Martin Bicknell. Terry Russell kindly provided drawings, and Brian Stocks assisted with the scanning of certain of the prints.

The poor quality of many of the images has to be accepted as a result of their age and poor copying in the past.

GEOGRAPHICAL SETTING

The site of the present city was chosen by the Romans for the building of a legionary fortress as a forward base for the conquest of Brigantia in the 70s AD, and the locality was named Deva. It was initially occupied by the 2nd Legion, and was a vital strongpoint with the advantage of easy supply by sea as it stood at the lowest practicable crossing of the River Dee. Originally constructed in turf and timber, the walls and buildings were rebuilt in stone in the 2nd century, when the base had attracted a considerable civilian community. In medieval times the walls were revamped on the old foundations, and their lower courses are the original Roman ones.

The city later thrived as a centre for traffic between England and North Wales, and for many centuries the Old Dee Bridge was the first crossing place over the river estuary. With the coming of the railways Chester became an important rail junction and a fine station was constructed in 1848, which still remains. The city is now a favourite tourist centre, with its many half-timbered buildings, 'rows' and gates. Many remnants of its Roman origins remain, including a large amphitheatre, and the famous Grosvenor Museum houses a fine collection of inscribed stonework from this period. The nearby museum of the Cheshire Regiment is also well worth a visit.

HISTORICAL BACKGROUND

The Chester horse tramway, which opened in June 1879, was laid to link the General Station, which was used by the GWR and LNWR with the city centre via City Road and Foregate, Eastgate and Bridge Streets to reach Grosvenor Street to cross the Dee and proceed to Saltney via Grosvenor Road, Hough Green and Chester Street, terminating near Saltney GWR station close to the Welsh border. The operator was the Chester Tramways Company, and the depot and stables were near the General Station. Though earlier historians have referred to the standard gauge line as single track, or have been vague as to its layout south-west of the city, the 1899 2nd Edition 25in/1:2500 Ordnance Survey map clearly shows that from the depot to Eastgate it was laid as double line. Along Eastgate Street and into Bridge Street it was single track with two turnouts, and then continued as double track as far as the Castle. Between the Castle and Saltney it remained single line with five passing loops. At Saltney a short length of single line ran beyond the terminal loop, ending opposite Curzon Street.

The original car fleet consisted of eight Eades patent reversible double deck trams, numbered 1-8, and probably built by Milnes in a livery of crimson lake and cream. Apparently these vehicles proved unsatisfactory and

were quickly replaced by eight one horse double deckers - seven constructed by a local coachbuilder and one by G.F. Milnes. Two Starbuck cars followed in 1885, again open top double deckers, followed by one built by the Company.

In 1886 Car 9 became the object of an experiment carried out by the local engineering firm of Hughes and Lancaster, who fitted it with a four cylinder compressed air engine powered by underfloor wrought iron cylinders. This pioneering contraption sadly suffered serious leakage problems, and in an effort to cure this deficiency, air feed mechanisms were fitted to the cast iron supply pipe, which was laid alongside the track, at certain points along the route. These feeders could be coupled to an automatic device under the tram to top up the air supply; when the vehicle restarted, the coupling disengaged and the feed was closed off. It would seem that the compressed air car only operated between Saltney and Grosvenor Bridge, and by 1890 was cut down to single deck format. The body of this singular tramcar survived until 1961 as a cricket pavilion at Acrefair near Wrexham.

By 1900 Chester Corporation was keen to purchase the horse line to electrify and extend it, and the following year it obtained an Act of Parliament to do so. On 1st January 1902 the line was purchased for £19,866 and the following November work began to relay it at a gauge of 3ft 6in/1067mm, commencing at the Station terminus. Horse car services ceased on 27th December, and the horses and car bodies sold off.

By the end of March 1903 twelve Milnes open top double deck electric trams, numbered 1-12, had been delivered to the rebuilt depot, in a livery of apple green and ivory, with gold and blue lining out. Mounted on 6ft/1.82metres Brill 21E four wheel trucks, the cars were hardly cutting edge, having the open platforms and short upper canopies which were out-of-date even by that time. They were exceptionally small vehicles, some of the most diminutive ever built for an English tramway and only seated 43 - 20 in the lower saloon, and 23 on the exposed upper deck. Originally no indicator boxes were fitted, and the legend GENERAL RAILWAY STATION & SALTNEY was painted above the cant rail.

The newly laid line followed the old route but was doubled throughout, save along Eastgate Street, where it was single track with one turnout. At Saltney the line was extended some 77 yards/70.4metres as far as Wood Street and the railway bridge which crossed Chester Street at this point. From the General Station as far as Eastgate the overhead was carried on ornate central poles; through the city centre the span wires were attached to buildings via rosettes, some of which still survive on shop frontages in the city centre, whilst from Grosvenor Street to Saltney, centre poles again took over, apart from Grosvenor Bridge to Overleigh Corner, where curious bracket posts with short arms each carrying one wire were set up on either side of the thoroughfare, though these were soon replaced with twin poles and span wire. In the 1920s, increasing traffic volume led to the replacement of all the centre posts with side ones lacking the ornamental wrought ironwork of the earlier examples.

In 1906 an eastern extension was commenced, running from Foregate Street along Boughton Road as far as Boughton Post Office, where the track forked, one branch running along Tarvin Road as far as the Bridge Inn, the other heading along Christleton Road to Stocks Lane. Both branches were laid as single track, with two passing loops on the former road, and one on the latter. The Boughton Road overhead was carried on twin poles and span wire, whilst the Tarvin and Christleton Road extensions relied on single bracket arm poles. Both new routes were opened on 22nd November 1906, and to cope with the extra traffic a 20 seat one man operated demi-car (No.13) was purchased from Brush that same year together with five open top cars (14-18) from UEC. These latter trams were exact copies of the earlier Milnes vehicles, apart from their electrical equipment and minor design differences. Car 13 was not a success, as it needed a conductor to keep to schedule, and after an unsuccessful attempt to sell it in late 1907 it was relegated to a variety of duties including a stint as a snow plough.

The tramway settled down to a quiet existence, with no additions to the car fleet, and no serious accidents. During the 1920s track, overhead and vehicles were gradually allowed to wear themselves out. Internal corrosion in the latter led to a variety of noises as they rumbled through the streets, and the locals were wont to refer to them as 'Julius Caesar's Chariots'! A March 1928 report recommended the substitution of motorbuses for trams, which the Council subsequently endorsed by a single vote. The Chester Corporation Act of 1929 empowered the city to run its own bus fleet, and the final tram, car 10, ran its last journey on the damp evening of 15th February 1930, packed inside and out.

HORSE CARS

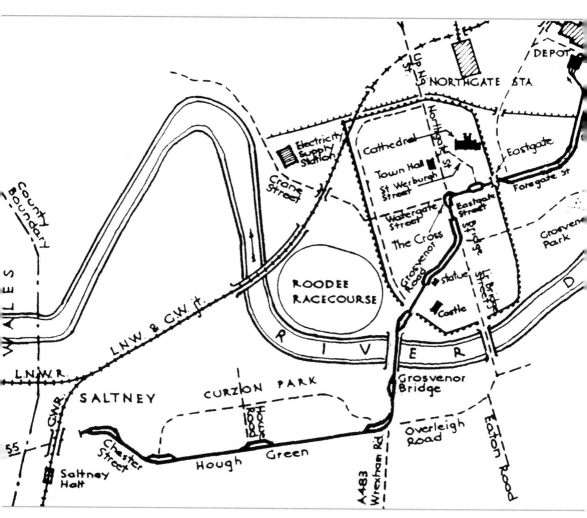

1.   The horse car route, inaugurated in 1879, ran in a south-westerly direction from the General Station to the suburb of Saltney, through the city centre. It was part double line, and part single with passing loops, and 2.38 miles long.

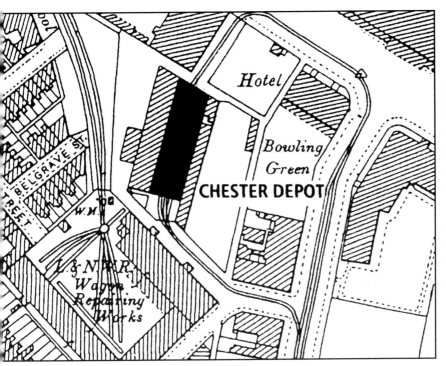

DEPOT

2. The depot and stables was situated across the road from the station which can be seen at top right. Trams entered the shed via a single line along Tramway Street and exited along Car Street, operating a one way system clockwise along this route.

3.   A superb, image of the horse tramshed, with crews and depot staff posing in front of the vehicles. The roof of the shed was later raised several feet to accommodate the electric cars (via M. Rowlands).

EASTGATE STREET

4.   Circa 1885, a pair of horse cars ply for trade along Eastgate Street having just negotiated the turnout. Note that the Eastgate has not yet acquired its ornate Jubilee clock and pedestrians include a lady fending off the sun with a parasol.

5.   A fine study depicts one of the trams taking the single line along the street beyond the loop and being pulled by two horses instead of the usual one. The presence of the Eastgate clock shows the photograph was taken after 1897.

6.   Another pre-1897 image of the street clearly showing the passing loop being traversed by a single tram. The thoroughfare must have been fairly well thronged at times judging by the variety of horse drawn traffic parked up on the right (via Chester Record Office).

7.   Taken from the top of the Eastgate on a sunny day, this shot picks out the loop with a single car awaiting passengers, plus a fine vista of the roadway flanked by a series of imposing buildings. Newgate Street is visible on the left, and St Werburgh Street on the right.

THE CROSS

8.   A horse tram heads along Eastgate Street, with St Peter's Church behind the car. In the foreground is the entrance to Bridge Street, seen on a busy summer day.

BRIDGE STREET

9.   Horse Car 10, pulled by a single beast, proceeds into the city along the thoroughfare, passing Commonhall Street on the left, and the Old Vaults hostelry. The picturesque buildings above the tram were known as the Dutch Houses. The double track can be clearly seen in the stone setts paving the street.

10.   Car 1 heads in the same direction as it approaches the Cross, with St Peter's Church forming an appropriate backdrop.

11.   At the southern end of the street Car 3 turns right into Grosvenor Street, with the entrance to White Friars visible on the left. The Meadows Frost drinking fountain topped by a streetlamp was erected in 1859 when that worthy, a local mill owner, was mayor of the city.

GROSVENOR STREET

12.   A poor photograph, but of interest, as it shows a horse tram with Chester Castle in the background and the spire of St Mary's Church across the River Dee just discernible above the animal.

SALTNEY TERMINUS

13.   Horse car 2 poses at the terminus with Curzon Street on the right. The vehicle had transverse upper deck seating fitted in the 1890s. Note the youthful conductor, and the advertisements fixed to the staircase risers.

14.   A well loaded Horse car 4 is pictured at the same venue, again with a youngster forming one of the crew. The two equines include a trace horse deemed necessary on this part of the route. The photograph shows good detail of the livery, including the waist panel number, and the destination painted on the rocker and dash panel.

15.   Tickets issued on the horse trams, printed by Williamsons, and showing no fare stages. The 2d example is pink, the 3d one white.

AIR PRESSURE EXPERIMENTS

16.   The original design of car 9 in its guise as a compressed air powered vehicle, shows the route it travelled and the driver preparing to collect a further air supply from the pipe laid alongside the track.

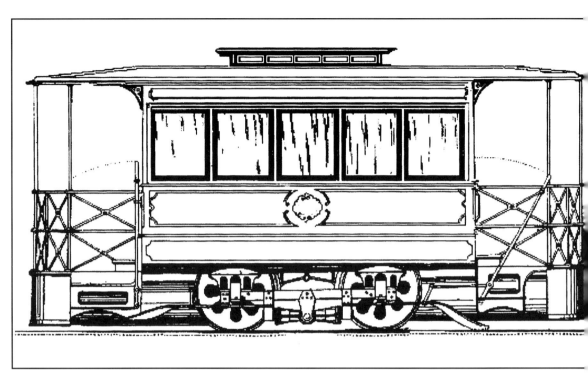

17.   The same car is illustrated as modified around 1890. Amazingly the vehicle, together with its still intact mechanism, survived as a cricket pavilion near Wrexham until 1961.

TRAMCAR DETAILS			
Fleet Number	1–12	13	14–18
Builder	Milnes Hadley, Salop	Brush, Loughborough	U.E.C.Co. Preston
Seating	20 lower, 23 upper deck	20	20 lower, 23 upper deck
Date in Service	April 1903	August 1906	1907
Length overall	25ft. 0in	22ft. 6in	25ft. 0in
Length of Platforms	5ft. 0in	5ft. 3in	5ft. 0in
Length of Saloon	14ft. 0in	11ft. 0in	14ft. 0in
Width overall	6ft. 3in	6ft. 3in	6ft. 3in
Height inside	6ft. 9in	7ft 6in	6ft. 9in
Height, Rail to trolley Plank	9ft. 11½in	10ft. 9½in	9ft. 11 5/8in
Trucks (6ft 0in wheelbase)	Brill 21E single	Brush Special	Brill 21E single
Diameter of Wheels	30 inch	31¾ inch	30 inch
Motors	2 x GE-58 25 hp	Brush	2 x Brush 1002B 25 hp
Controllers	B.18	Raworth	B.18

ELECTRIC CARS

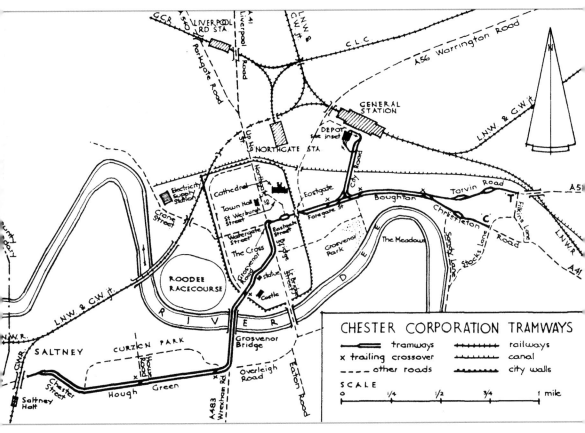

18.   The electric cars followed the course of the old horse trams, though the track was doubled almost throughout its length. In 1906 an eastern extension was laid along Boughton Road, forking to serve Tarvin and Christleton Roads (after H.G. Dibdin).

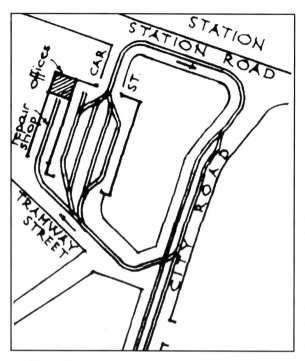

19.   The depot was enlarged to accommodate the electric trams, with a repair shop provided on the west side. The junction from City Road into Tramway Street was also modified at this time (after H.G. Dibdin).

20.   The frontage of the electricity generating station built on New Crane Street in 1896. Power from the works was used to run the tramway.

21.   The façade of the station offices shows the date of its erection. It is obvious that this new facility encouraged the council to consider electrifying the system.

GENERAL STATION

→

22.　　A photograph of an early electric tram trial shows car 5 at the north end of City Road with the station behind. The Queen Hotel, once the biggest building in the city, stands on the right, and the usual crowd of youngsters has gathered to stare at the cameraman.

→

23.　　Car 11 is pictured at the same place, with the Albion Hotel (now the Town Crier) on the left. The imposing frontage of the station, built in 1848 in Italianate style in dark brick shows up well behind the tram. The lack of a destination box shows the image to be an early one in the history of the service.

→

24.　　Car 2 is also depicted at the station terminus, a summer photograph judging by the motorman's white topped cap, and post First World War according to the cars parked in the distance. Note the indicator box showing SALTNEY as the vehicle's destination.

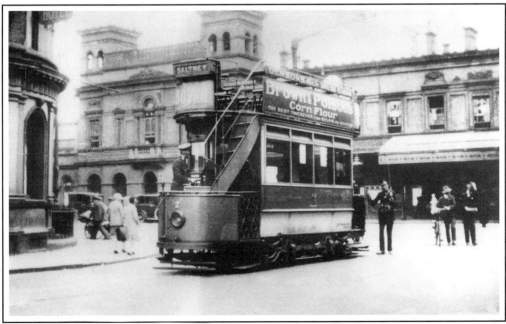

25.   An end-of-service shot at the same venue shows car 9, in its final livery, as it picks up trade for Saltney. The motorman poses for the camera, whilst the elegant lady on the right makes a fashion statement in cloche hat and short skirt. Note that bracket poles carry the overhead round the front of the station.

26.   Demi-car 13 halts in front of the Albion Hotel. This photograph shows clearly the long frontage of the General Station with its line of parked carriages. The long trolley boom of the single decker occasionally caused dewirement problems, which were never satisfactorily solved.

CHESTER CORPORATION ELECTRIC TRAMWAYS

Timetable 1921-1922

General Station to Saltney

Monday to Friday – 6-10, 6-35, 7, 7-30, 7-40, 8 a.m. then every 7½ minutes until 8 p.m. ; then every 10 minutes until 10-30 p.m.

Saturday – As above until 11 a.m. then every 6 minutes until 9 p.m. ; then every 7½ minutes until 10-45 p.m.

Sunday – 9-45 a.m. ; then every 20 minutes until 3 p.m. ; then every 8 minutes until 9-56 p.m.

Bank Holidays – Cars run as Saturdays, first car leaving Station at 7-40 a.m.

Good Friday – Cars run as Sundays.

Saltney to General Station

Monday to Friday – 6-35, 5-55, 7-20, 7-40, 8, 8-15, 8-27 a.m. then every 7½ minutes until 8-20 p.m. ; then every 10 minutes until 10-50 p.m.

Saturday – As above until 11-20 a.m. then every 6 minutes until 9-20 p.m. ; then every 7½ minutes until 11-5 p.m.

Sunday – 10-5 a.m. ; then every 20 minutes until 3-5 p.m. ; then every 8 minutes until 10-16 p.m.

Bank Holidays – Cars run as Saturdays, first car leaving Saltney at 8 a.m.

Good Friday – Cars run as Sundays.

Boughton Routes

Monday to Friday – Tarvin Road to St. Werburgh Street – 7, 8 a.m. then every 20minutes until 10-20 p.m. ; St. Werburgh Street to Tarvin Road – 6-50, 7-50 a.m. then every 20minutes until 10-30 p.m. ; Christleton Road to St. Werburgh Street – 7-10 a.m. then every 20 minutes until 10-30 p.m. ; St. Werburgh Street to Christleton Road – 7- a.m. then every 20minutes until 10-40 p.m. ;

Saturday – As above, with an additional car between Tarvin Road and St. Werburgh Street, leaving Tarvin Road at 12-5 p.m. then every 20 minutes until 10:25 p.m. and leaving St. Werburgh Street at 12-15 p.m. and then every 20 minutes until 10-35 p.m.

Sunday – Tarvin Road to St. Werburgh Street – 10 a.m. then every 40 minutes until 2-40 p.m. then 3 p.m. and every 20 minutes until 9-40 p.m. ; St. Werburgh Street to Tarvin Road – 10-30 a.m. then every 40minutes until 2-30 p.m. then 2-50 p.m. and every 20 minutes until 9-50 p.m. ; Christleton Road to St. Werburgh Street – 10-20 a.m. then every 40 minutes until 2-20 p.m. then 3-10 p.m. and every 20 minutes until 9-50 p.m. ; St. Werburgh Street to Christleton Road – 10-10- a.m. then every 40minutes until 2-10 p.m. then 3 p.m. and every 20 minutes until 10 p.m.

Bank Holidays – Cars run as weekdays, from Tarvin Road 8 a.m., from Christleton Road 8-10 a.m.

Good Friday – Cars run as Sundays.

CITY ROAD

27.   A view of the thoroughfare taken in the 1920s after the centre poles had been replaced with twin standards and span wire. The twin tracks were laid in granite setts, and roadworks are clearly in progress. Opposite the steamroller was the temperance Stafford Hotel, one of many establishments catering for visitors.

28.   Car 6, on its way to the station, crosses the Shropshire Union Canal over the road bridge at the same point as picture 27. This 1929 image illustrates the dilapidated state of the vehicles in the last few months of service.

29.   Car 12 is here seen at the south end of the street on its way to Saltney, a view which picks out the centre poles, many of which were crowned with streetlamps. Note the triangular track junction, which took trams left onto Foregate Street or right to Boughton. The verandah of the Royalty Theatre, whose advertisement appears in picture 27, can be seen to the right of the car. The establishment was built in 1882 and staged variety programmes until its closure in 1966.

FOREGATE STREET

30.   Tracklaying is taking place along the street, a scene perhaps relating to repairs or relaying in the 1920s, as the trees, in full leaf, argue against the original construction, which took place between November 1902 and March 1903 (via J. Clowes).

31.   The north side of the street looking towards City Road, a view which shows well the central poles with their short bracket arms, and the twin tracks running on either side of the stanchions which were painted in brown and cream.

32.   Looking towards Eastgate Street, this vista shows well the centre pole and twin track arrangement in this part of the city with the White Lion on the right. Note that the whole width of the thoroughfare was paved with stone setts. This card was posted in 1926 with the communication written in French!

33.   A scene photographed from the opposite side of the road, with Eastgate visible in the distance and car 12 heading for Saltney. A primitive looking motorbus can be seen alongside a passing cart, whilst a young lady walks her dog on the pavement at the bottom right.

34.   Another Foregate Street scene with the building next door to the White Lion advertising Humber motor vehicles. Beneath the sign is an open top tourer, whilst car 3 halts at the stop on its way into the city.

35.   Taken from the top of Eastgate, this 1920s view looks back along Foregate Street with various vehicles including a motorbus jockeying for position. In the near distance is a tramcar. The tramlines and overhead can be clearly picked out in this picture.

36.   A scene taken from Foregate Street, shows car 9 easing its way under the Eastgate arch. St John Street is on the left, and on the right a GWR dray has just collected a barrel from Chester Northgate Brewery Office, now W.H. Smith's bookshop.

37.   Shot from the opposite direction this fine study shows car 1 passing under the arch into Foregate Street on a wet and dreary day. The conductor eyes the young lady cyclist as she pedals by. The previous picture was taken from the corner by Blossom's Hotel, seen on the right. There was much discussion about top-covering the trams, but it was considered doubtful whether they could pass under the arch. Judging by this image, it would have been just about feasible.

EASTGATE STREET

38.   Looking down Eastgate Street from Eastgate, one of the trams comes off the loop on its way under the arch. Both overhead wiring and the tramlines show up well in the sunshine. Between Eastgate and the Cross the thoroughfare was paved with woodblocks, the only part of the route so surfaced.

39.   Looking from the opposite direction along a thinly populated street, cars 8 and 10 stand side-by-side on the turnout. The former is heading for the station, the latter to Saltney. Note the line of elegant half timbered shops on the right, with steps leading up to the first floor enclosed 'rows'.

40.   Another excellent shot reveals cars 8 (in the distance) and 2, both stationary on the loop, with an open topped motor car on the left. The pedestrians are well worth examining, and at centre left we note a pair of giant spectacles advertising H.C. Houghton's opticians. The card was posted in 1911.

41.   In the narrow streets of the city centre the span wires were fixed to buildings by rosettes, and the stop signs were likewise fastened to any convenient support. The signs were all tinplate enamel, red letters on white for compulsory stops, blue on white for requests. Above the sign, a pair of *pince-nez* advertise Siddall's Opticians.

42.   Car 3 halts opposite on the loop opposite St Werburgh Street, whilst the conductor helps a young child to disembark from the upper deck. Note the two ladies strolling in front of the tram in their Sunday best, whilst overhead and span wire show up well in the shot.

43. A poor photograph, but worth including, as it shows Chester during the May Race Week, with Eastgate Street thronged with busy crowds and every tram, including the single decker, pressed into service for the occasion. The well filled vehicles are heading for the Roodee racecourse via Bridge and Grosvenor Streets.

44. Taken from the opposite side of the roadway, three trams, with car 13 sandwiched between two double deckers, move in line towards the Roodee. The nearest vehicle carries the legend RACES ONLY in its destination box.

45.   We observe another quiet day in the street, with a distant tram moving under Eastgate arch, and an excellent view of the overhead, supported on span wires. A set of guard wires can also be made out around the nearest pair of frogs.

46.   The eyes still have it on the left, as a single tram heads for the General Station in this study taken before World War 1. Dutton's grocers on the left boasts 'the sign of the Roman altar', whilst the fashionable Bolland's Resturant can be seen on the extreme right.

47.   A good shot of the little demi-car, pressed into service for the Race traffic in May 1912. The indicator box, showing THE FOUNTAIN BOUGHTON has been hidden by a paper sticker reading TO RACES.

48.   Eastgate Street is shown *en fete* in this postwar photograph with two trams, including car 11 waiting on the loop. The proliferation of British and Commonwealth flags decorating all the buildings is perhaps connected with celebrations relating to the peace.

49.　　Two trams can be seen in this view, the rearmost waiting on the loop whilst car 11 in the foreground is moving along the single line on its way to Saltney. In this busy scene Cash's bootmakers on the left are holding a 'great clearance sale' whilst Richard Jones's premises, above the far cyclist, was a mercers and clothiers. On the right a row of buckets can be seen above Shaw's ironmongers.

50.　　A fine study shows car 3 approaching the Cross in the first year of the electric tram service. Note the lack of a destination box, and the wire netting surrounding the top deck. The city crest is carried on the waist panel, with the Corporation logo on the rocker below.

51.   Seen from Watergate Street, one of the new trams is about to turn left into Bridge Street on this busy corner, with St Peter's Church visible on the left. On both sides of the street can be seen the 'rows' which allowed covered access to the shops at first-floor level.

52.   A view replicated many times in postcard images, the corner by the Cross, the axis of the city, was constructed in 1888 to designs by T.M. Lockwood. In this study dating from 1905 one of the trams has halted by the stop before joining the double track which can be seen in front of the vehicle.

53.   A good picture of the thinly populated corner depicts car 8 posed for the cameraman. The image shows clearly the steps leading up to the railed first storey passages, and though obviously dating to the early years of the tramway, this postcard was not mailed until 1928.

54.   An excellent shot of the double track, which opens out from single on the turning from Eastgaste Street into Bridge Street. The distant motor cars and the soldier in front of the steps on the right suggest a First World War date for the photograph. The cart on the left has its offside wheel in the tramline, a trick often used by such vehicles to ease their passage, much to the detriment of the track itself!

BRIDGE STREET

55.   A tramcar pauses on the double line on the thoroughfare in this southward looking scene. On the right a street sweeper keeps the area clear of horse droppings and other dirt, whilst the tower of St Michael's Church can be seen in the right hand distance.

56.   In this 1922 picture the increase in traffic density can be well appreciated as car 15 heads inward towards the Cross. The conductor on the rear platform keeps a watching brief on events.

57.   At the southern end of the street the twin track curves left into Grosvenor Street in this animated scene, as a lone tramcar moves towards the city centre. In this colour postcard the vehicle was depicted in a fetching red livery!

58.　　　Car 4 and passengers pause to have their picture taken at the southern corner of the thoroughfare under the watchful eye of the inspector behind the tram. Advertising boards have appeared along the upper deck, whilst the ladder on the right might be part of the tower wagon. St Michael's Church on the far right is now the premises of the History and Heritage Centre.

GROSVENOR STREET

59.   Looking back towards the corner of Bridge Street, the previous picture was taken just behind the distant centre pole. The twin tracks show up well, and to the right of the horse and cart can be seen the Frost Meadows drinking fountain.

60.   Further south-west along the same street was the imposing Franciscan Church and Monastery. The centre bracket poles and double track continued along this thoroughfare.

————▶

61.   Looking north-east in this snowy scene, a tram heads towards Saltney. The Fransiscan Church is on the left, whilst to the right is the imposing frontage of the Grosvenor Museum with its fine turreted clock. The image gives good detail of the lines and overhead at this point. The lady on the left seems to be struggling with an oversized umbrella!

————▶

62.   A much more summery view as car 11 runs inbound in this 1908 shot which reveals a road completely devoid of other traffic.

GROSVENOR ROAD

63.   With the Grosvenor Museum in the left background, car 10 heads for Saltney, passing the imposing equestrian statue of Sir Stapleton Cotton, First Viscount Combermere, sited outside the castle. Sculpted by Marochetti, the statue was erected in 1865 to commemorate the viscount, a professional soldier who served in the Peninsular War and India. Again the photograph clearly shows the layout of track and standards at this point (via F. Simpson).

64.   The same location as the previous view, but it now shows car 11 heading in the opposite direction. The trolley booms of the double deck cars were offset, as can be seen in this and other shots, resulting in a longer traverse when the pole was on the nearside of the vehicle.

65.   One of the electric cars crosses Grosvenor Bridge, with the twin bracket poles in use on this part of the line just visible, and the castle in sight under the arch. Strong winds occasionally blew across the river, and conductors were instructed to keep control over the trolley ropes over this section, whilst motormen were warned not to stop on the bridge under any circumstances.

66.   Car 11 poses on the southern approach to the bridge, showing that with the appearance of upper deck advertisements, the destination board has been moved to the top of the rail. Crew and inspector all wear the kepi style caps then in vogue, with single breasted coats sporting a single line of buttons. In the background can be seen the row of short bracket arm poles carrying single wires in use on this part of the route. These caused difficulties with the trolley heads and were later replaced with twin poles and span wire.

⟶

67.   This vista shows the lower sweep of Grosvenor Road by the entrance to Overleigh Cemetery, with car 6 halted for the camera. The photograph shows again the unusual short arm poles then used on this part of the route, and a stop sign on the standard on the right, above the bearded ancient evidently welcoming the new era in urban transport.

⟶

68.   Car 6 and another tram pass each other at a sylvan Overleigh Corner in the summer of 1905 on one of the sharpest curves along the line. Here centre poles have taken over from the twin posts. Another stop sign can be seen on the right hand pole which stands at the entrance to Hough Green.

69.   An excellent side view of car 2 at Overleigh Corner, with Hough Green situated on the left. By this time indicator boxes have appeared on the vehicles. Note the external brake and the wrought iron gate joining the dash panel to the car body at the rear.

HOUGH GREEN

70.   Around 1925 the tram track along Hough Green was repaired and partly relaid. This photograph shows the replacement rails forming the Overleigh Corner curve laid out near the bridge (seen at top left), before they were placed in position.

71.   Car 11, an obvious favourite with local cameramen, pauses by the Howe Road crossover, seen behind the tram, on its way into the city. This wide and attractive boulevard was being built up at this time, and many fine houses lined its northern side. Again, centre poles carried the overhead as far as Saltney terminus.

72.   Another view of the thoroughfare with a delivery boy posed between the tracks and an approaching tram. It is a moot point whether this part of the line ever paid for itself. It was at this time fairly sparsely occupied, with the only population concentrated at the Saltney suburb.

73.   The 1925 repairs were quite extensive; here workmen seal off the inside of the rails with hot tar.

←————

74.　　Another shot depicts line relaying with the tie bars separating the rails clearly visible. Note the setts being replaced on the left.

←————

75.　　This picture of Hough Green is taken looking towards Saltney, with open fields still in evidence on the south side of the roadway. The left hand line has evidently been completed, whilst in the foreground the careful task of placing the setts is under way. By this time the central poles had been replaced with twin poles and span wire. In the distance a tram heads for the terminus.

76.　　At the eastern end of the Green the line curves into Chester Street, with the newly completed Clivedon Road leading off to the left in front of the substantial house boasting twin chimneys. Behind the distant right hand pole one building is still in the process of completion.

SALTNEY TERMINUS

77.   Car 12 is at the terminus at the start of the electric service with crew and inspector in uniform wearing the quasi-military kepi style hats in vogue at this time. No advertisements are yet in evidence, and the top deck garden seats have not yet been swung for the return journey. Note that the upper deck front seats face backwards.

78.   Another fine early study, this time of car 6 at Saltney manned by another crew. The man in civvies on the left may be a Milnes official. The details of the little tram show up to perfection, including the short canopy and the steep staircase.

79.   Car 2 is at Saltney, with the GWR railway bridge behind, and the City Arms public house on the right, next door to the post office and newsagents. The advertisement of the 'annual sale' on the right dates the postcard to January 1905.

80.   A close up of the same tram reveals a posing crew and the terminal pole behind the car. The Welsh border is marked by the post just behind the young lad in the middle distance.

81.	Looking in the opposite direction, car 3 is the subject of this study, with a good view of the City Arms and the last pole of the terminus. The trolley boom has already been swung for the return journey.

82.	The cameraman has here utilised the railway bridge for his exposure, again revealing one of the trams on the final stretch of single line beyond the distant twin track. Wood Street can be seen on the right and Curzon Street at left centre.

83.   Near the end of the tram service a worse-for-wear car 16 and its crew pose at Saltney during the final summer of operations.

BOUGHTON ROAD

84.　　　Along the Boughton Road extension the overhead was supported on twin poles and span wire, instead of the more usual centre posts. This view looks east with St Paul's Church on the right; the chimneys belong to houses on Barrow Well Hill. On the distant left is Boughton Post Office where the line bifurcated along Tarvin and Christleton Roads.

85.   The mock half timbered Post Office building is flanked on the left by Tarvin Road, with car 10 bound for the terminus, and Christleton Road to the right part blocked by car 2.

86.   Tarvin Road utilised bracket poles to carry the overhead. In front of car 10 an inspector keeps a wary eye on proceedings.

87.   The Union flag can be seen fluttering on the offside top deck of Car 2 as part of a short lived experiment to identify Boughton bound trams, together with the board hung on the dash which read ST WERBURGH ST AND TARVIN (OR CHRISTLETON) ROAD. The flapping ensigns tended to shy passing horses, and the ill-starred flags and boards were soon replaced with destination boxes.

88.   Another shot of the junction clearly shows the track divergence, and a stop sign on the left hand pole. Car 5 still carries the flag and dash board, whilst the posing pedestrians may represent passengers waiting to board the vehicle!

89.   Blizzard conditions prevail at Bougton, as an unidentified tram battles the elements on its way into the city. In such weather open platform cars made life near impossible for motormen who were completely exposed to the elements. Very sensibly the conductor is doubtless sheltering inside the saloon with the passengers. Trams could generally operate fairly happily in such circumstances as long as the track remained swept and the overhead wire stayed free of ice.

90.   Latter days at the same venue, with one of the little 1-12 series cars showing off its final livery. Note the route board in the side window, and the good view of the Brill truck and wrought iron gate joining dash panel and car body. The small size of these Milnes vehicles is well illustrated in this view.

CHRISTLETON ROAD

91.   An excellent study depicts car 1 and crew at Christleton terminus after the fitting of indicator boxs and a red-painted metal letter 'C' fixed at either end of the top deck of the tram for further identification of the destination. Note the feeder cable supplying power to the overhead wires above the vehicle.

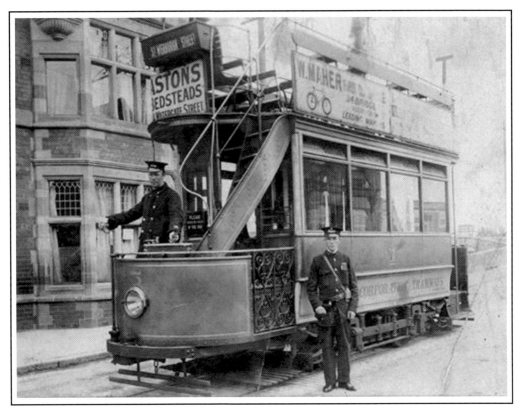

92.   Car 3 is outside the Bridge Inn at the terminus, this time displaying a metal 'T' above the indicator box. As the destination shows, Boughton trams commenced running from St Werburgh Street in the city centre. Again the photograph shows good detail of the salient features of the vehicle.

93.	This view clearly shows the terminal track on Tarvin Road, with the Bridge Inn on the left and Stocks Lane off to the right. It was intended to link both Boughton termini, but the union never took place. The absence of any poles and overhead suggests this image was taken after the service ended and the equipment removed.

ORDINARY ADULT FARES ON THE CORPORATION TRAMWAYS

Section	Pre-1917	Mar. 1917	May 1918	April 1919	Feb. 1921	Feb. 1923	Mar. 1927
General Railway Station to St. Werburgh Street	1d	1d	1d	1½d	2d	1½d	1d
St. Werburgh Street to Boughton, Fountain	1d	1d	1d	1½d	2d	1½d	1d
St. Werburgh Street to Christleton Road or Tarvin Road Terminus	1d	1d	1½d	1½d	2d	1½d	1½d
General Railway Station to Castle	1d	1½d	1½d	1½d	2d	1½d	1½d
General Railway Station to Overleigh Road	2d	2d	2d	2d	2½d	2d	2d
General Railway Station to Saltney	2d	2½d	3d	3d	4d	3d	3d

LAST DAY

94.   The last tram, car 10, suitably thronged with passengers including civic dignitaries and boys from a local orphanage, clanks up Grosvenor Street on the wet evening of 15th February 1930, whilst a replacing motorbus on the left heads for Saltney. The boys hung an appropriate funeral wreath which can be seen halfway down the trolley boom.

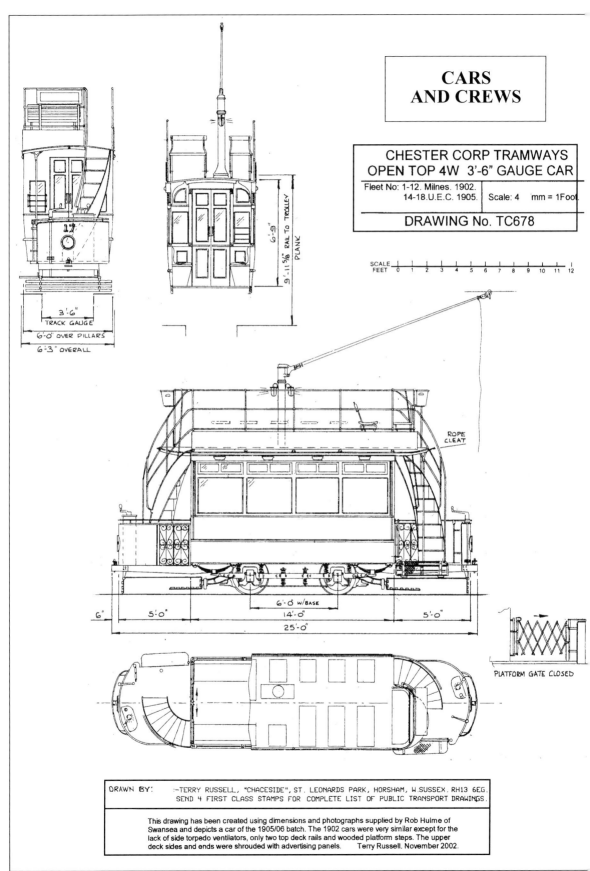

CARS
AND CREWS

CHESTER CORP TRAMWAYS
OPEN TOP 4W 3'-6" GAUGE CAR

| Fleet No: 1-12. Milnes. 1902. | |
| 14-18.U.E.C. 1905. | Scale: 4   mm = 1Foot. |

DRAWING No. TC678

SCALE
FEET 0 1 2 3 4 5 6 7 8 9 10 11 12

9'-11⁵/₆ RAIL TO TROLLEY PLANK

6'-9"

ROPE CLEAT

3'-6"
TRACK GAUGE
6'-0" OVER PILLARS
6'-3" OVERALL

6"   5'-0"   6'-0 w/BASE   14'-0"   5'-0"
25'-0"

PLATFORM GATE CLOSED

DRAWN BY: :-TERRY RUSSELL, "CHACESIDE", ST. LEONARDS PARK, HORSHAM, W.SUSSEX. RH13 6EG.
SEND 4 FIRST CLASS STAMPS FOR COMPLETE LIST OF PUBLIC TRANSPORT DRAWINGS.

This drawing has been created using dimensions and photographs supplied by Rob Hulme of Swansea and depicts a car of the 1905/06 batch. The 1902 cars were very similar except for the lack of side torpedo ventilators, only two top deck rails and wooded platform steps. The upper deck sides and ends were shrouded with advertising panels.   Terry Russell. November 2002.

← ———— 95. This three-view drawing is of one of the 1906 UEC built double deckers (14-18) which differed from the 1-12 Milnes vehicles only in minor details. The 6ft Brill truck ensured a hard ride, and the offset trolley pole can be clearly seen.

96. One of the UEC cars seen before delivery. Design differences included scoop ventilators along the cant rail, and square corners to the bulkhead doors instead of round.

97. The interior of car 14 as delivered. Original fittings included dark blue curtains, and the finish was in teak. Note the strap hangers and the pear shaped globes on the lamps.

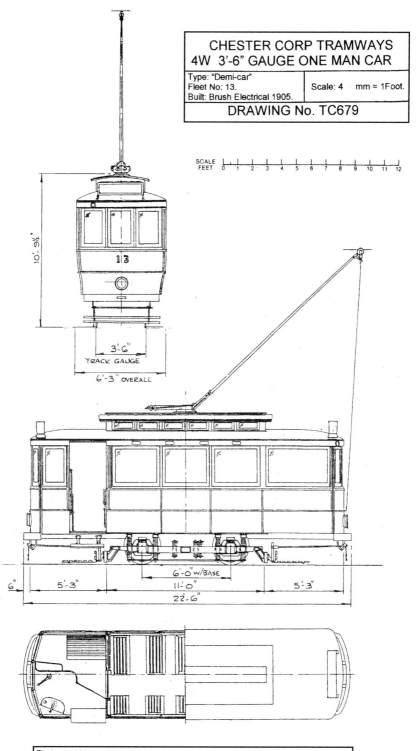

CHESTER CORP TRAMWAYS
4W 3'-6" GAUGE ONE MAN CAR

Type: "Demi-car"
Fleet No: 13.
Built: Brush Electrical 1905.

Scale: 4 mm = 1Foot.

DRAWING No. TC679

SCALE
FEET 0 1 2 3 4 5 6 7 8 9 10 11 12

10'-9½"

3'-6"
TRACK GAUGE

6'-3" OVERALL

6'-0" W/BASE

11'-0"

22'-6"

6"

5'-3"

5'-3"

The basis of this drawing was of a Maidstone car created by Robert Harley and I have modified it using dimensions and photographs supplied by Rob Hulme of Swansea.
Terry Russell. November 2002.

DRAWN BY:- ROBERT HARLEY/TERRY RUSSELL AND KINDLY MADE AVAILABLE THROUGH:-
TERRY RUSSELL, "CHACESIDE", ST. LEONARDS PARK, HORSHAM, W.SUSSEX. RH13 6EG.
SEND 4 FIRST CLASS STAMPS FOR COMPLETE LIST OF PUBLIC TRANSPORT DRAWINGS.

←——— 98.   A three view drawing of Brush Demi-car 13, shows the neat appearance of this little all enclosed vehicle, with its 6ft wheelbase truck and clerestory roof.

99.   Car 13 is shown in the depot yard, showing GENERAL STATION on its destination box. Note the FRONT EXIT AND ENTRANCE sign in the front window.

100.   A good side view of the same tram, again at the depot, shows the entrance door and the livery it carried in its latter years.

101.   In the tramshed car 13 has a snowplough attached to one end. Unsuccessful as a service vehicle, the little demi-car performed various duties, including a stint as a stores van. At the end of the tramway period it was considered the soundest tram in the fleet! (via Chester Record Office).

102. Few pictures are available of any decorated Chester trams, though this example, taken at the General Station, shows one of the UEC cars bedizened in patriotic vein for a recruiting drive in World War 1 with images of Lord Kitchener on the rocker panel. Was the wreathed portrait on the dash panel a tramway employee killed in the conflict?

103. An interesting study depicts car 5 at the station terminus awaiting trade for Saltney. The livery and local adverts place the period before World War 1.

104.   We observe a close up of one of the youthful horse
tram conductors busily filling in his waybill. Many horse car
undertakings employed youngsters such as these, presumably
as they were paid less than adult members of staff.

105.   By contrast Hilda Conway, who served on the trams during World War 1, is shown warmly wrapped in a suitable uniform, well-equipped with leggings, Bell punch, change bag and whistle (via J. Garner).

106.   One of the replacement bus fleet, AEC Regal single-decker No.3, waits at the General Station in April 1930. The tram tracks remain *in situ* on the left of the photograph.

107.   Tickets used on the electric trams - from left to right they include a 1d white and 2d blue, a child's ½d (orange with green overprint), a pale buff exchange ticket for Boughton section journeys involving a change of tram and a 1½d lilac example introduced at the end of World War 1.

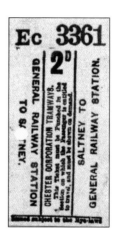

108.   Tokens were also issued on the tramway, including this blue 1d example.

109.   The lower saloon of Car 4 was purchased as a garden shed, and survived
for many years in this guise.

110.   The remnants of this vehicle were relocated in 2004 and have been stored for preservation. One of the bulkheads is being restored for display at the Wirral Transport Museum. This view shows the remains of the saloon end and the sliding door of the bulkhead (John Murray).

SURVIVALS

111.   Amazingly, much trackwork remains inside the premises of the old tram depot, which now houses the modern bus fleet. Along the rest of the route the tramlines were covered over with tarmacadam, though over the years most of the rails have subsequently been lifted. It is believed that the triangular junction at the south end of City Road still remains intact. This view shows Tramway Street which leads into the bus depot, though sadly no sign exists to indicate its historic name.

112.   A fine stretch of single tramline, laid in well-preserved setts, can be seen at the entrance to the depot yard, unused for some 77 years.

113.   Looking in the opposite direction, the distant motorbus is just entering the depot along Tramway Street. Two sets of facinf points lead off the length of single line towards the old tramshed and repair shop.

114.   Here the surviving tracks can be clearly seen as the spur lines curve away. The first two lead into the depot, the distant one to the repair facilities.

115.   The rear of the old tramshed is now a home for the Chester bus fleet. The roof of this building had to be raised to accommodate the electric trams, and the tops of the buttresses show the brickwork of this elevation.

116.   Car Street, again bearing no street sign, shows a length of single track leading to the front of the old car shed, again laid in a bed of surviving setts.

117.　　Looking north along Car Street, this photograph picks out the frontage of the General Station, and shows the trailing set of points in the foreground. Tramcars used this line every morning on their way into service.

118.   The frontage of the car shed has hardly changed over the years, though no carved plaque indicates the structure's original purpose.

119.   Alongside the car shed are the original tramway offices, a little dilapidated, but still in everyday use.

120.   The interior of the tramshed as it appears today. In parts of the floor where the concrete is broken or eroded sections of tram track can still be made out.

MP Middleton Press

EVOLVING THE ULTIMATE RAIL ENCYCLOPEDIA

Easebourne Lane, Midhurst, West Sussex.
GU29 9AZ   Tel:01730 813169

www.middletonpress.co.uk   email:info@middletonpress.co.uk

A-0 906520 B-1 873793 C-1 901706 D-1 904474

OOP Out of print at time of printing - Please check availability BROCHURE AVAILABLE SHOWING NEW TITLES